Life doesn't
have to be
Perfect
to be
Wonderful!
♥
Randa
Cantor

you were born to
SHINE!
♥
Amanda
Kriesel

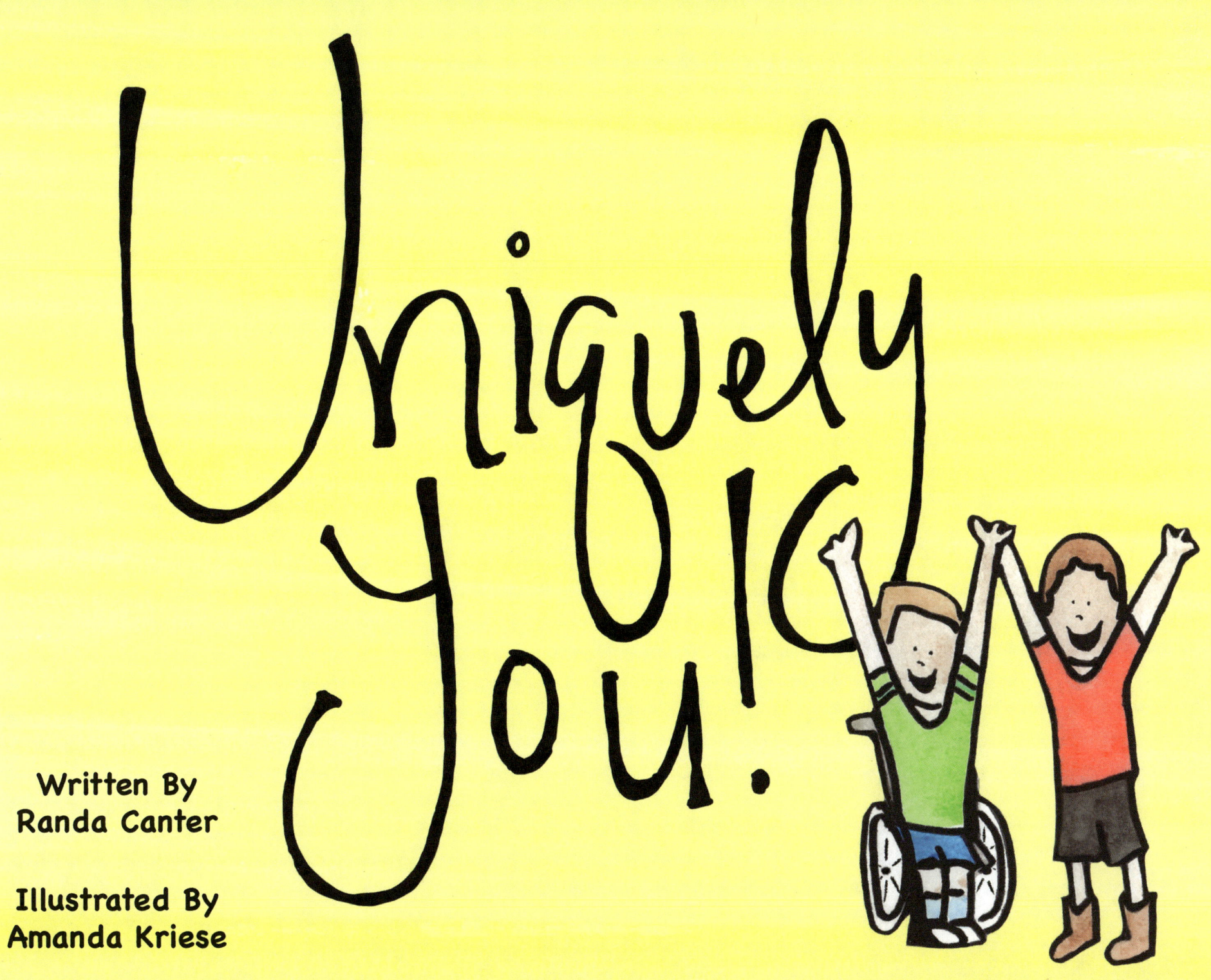

Uniquely You!

Written By
Randa Canter

Illustrated By
Amanda Kriese

I dedicate this book to God, who is my strength and has provided me eyes to see
His MIGHTY MIRACLES that many times have appeared as challenges in my life.
I will praise His name forever.
- Randa

It's been about discovering. My own hidden talent and God's hand in directing it.
So very thankful for all who were beside me in this journey. Nick's continual
encouragement, my children's desire to paint beside me, Randa's belief in me and
so many of you who cheered along the way. Thank you!
-Amanda

This edition first published in 2020
by Lawley Publishing,
a division of Lawley Enterprises LLC.

Published by Lawley Publishing
70 S. Val Vista Dr. #A3 #188
Gilbert, Az. 85296
www.LawleyPublishing.com

Let's work together to find and discover,
which things are alike and distinct from each other!

Listen and look, point them out as we read,
they build our character, it's just what we need!

Our uniqueness shows in each talent and skill.
We're all individual, it makes living a thrill!

There's something special in everyone - IT'S TRUE!
No mystery about it, you're Uniquely You!

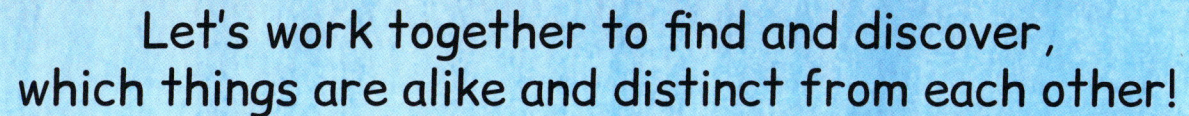

Come meet two new friends,
they'll be our cool guides!
They'll teach us how life
can be a SWEET ride!

Parker loves popping wheelies
and rolling in style,
while cheering on the Packers
with his GIANT smile!

Crew loves stomping in boots
and wearing tall socks!
He has really fast feet
and at soccer HE ROCKS!

Both boys are alike
in so many ways,
but they're different too!
And that DESERVES PRAISE!

Parker enjoys a cool
dip in the water.
Swimming and splashing
as summer gets hotter.

Crew cannon-balls in!
Both boys swim like a fish.
Yet there is a difference
you WON'T want to miss.

Crew uses both arms AND legs
to move fast and dive down.
Parker uses ONLY his arms
to flip himself around.

It's good to be different!
It's AWESOME - you see?
That's exactly the way
it's supposed to be!

**What is different and
what is the same?**

These friends enjoy bouncing
for hours on the tramp.
Parker laughs as Crew kicks
and flips like a champ!

Parker's trampoline time
is spent on his bottom.
He crawls, rolls and wrestles
without any problem!

They find different ways
to jump and to fly.

One needs help from a
friend to bounce up high!

It's fun to find joy in
what others can do.

Even if it is something
you can't do too.

**What is different and
what is the same?**

First day of school

It's been a great summer
for Parker and Crew.
The school year is starting -
it's all so brand new.

Parker feels nervous.
Our friend Crew does not.
Their feelings are different.
Hmm... Give that some thought.

The first day was scary
for Parker – not Crew.

Why did they feel different?
How is it for you?

What is different and
what is the same?

They are in the same class
and both work HARD to learn.
Parker loves reading
but Crew passes his turn.

Crew loves to do math,
to add and subtract.
Their interests are different,
that's a SURE FACT.

They both work at their desks
to color and write.
Their minds are SO different
and wonderfully bright!

**What is different and
what is the same?**

Their tummies are GROWLING,
it's time for lunch.
They all get in line,
they are ready to munch.

LUNCH BOX

Parker uses his stander,
his food on a tray.
He eats lunch with his friends
in his own special way.

Crew and his classmates
sit on the bench to eat.
They do things uniquely,
and it's SUCH A TREAT!

What is different and
what is the same?

It's recess time!!!
They both race to the swings.

They do it different but
enjoy common things!

Crew jumps off the swing
and runs to kick a ball.

His legs are tired,
he feels like he could fall.

Crew asks Parker for a
turn to sit in his chair.
Parker's legs do not work.
He can't stand up to share.

Crew understands,
so he rests on a bench.
Parker waits with his friend,
it's such a cinch!

**What is different and
what is the same?**

Cc Dd Ee Ff Gg Hh Ii Jj Kk Ll Mm Nn Oo Pp Qq Rr Ss T

Some topics are private,
we don't share them out loud.
The restroom is a subject
not yelled in a crowd.

Crew's body tells him
he needs to "go" during class.
He raises his hand;
the teacher gives him a pass.

Parker's body can't tell him when he needs to "go".
Scheduled times and helpers are required to know.

Even though their bodies work in different ways,
these friends choose to be kind to each other, ALWAYS!

**What is different and
what is the same?**

We all use soap and water
to clean our hands.
It's a great tool to wash
away germs and sand.

Some friends may need medicine
or other neat tools,
like devices to help them
communicate at school.

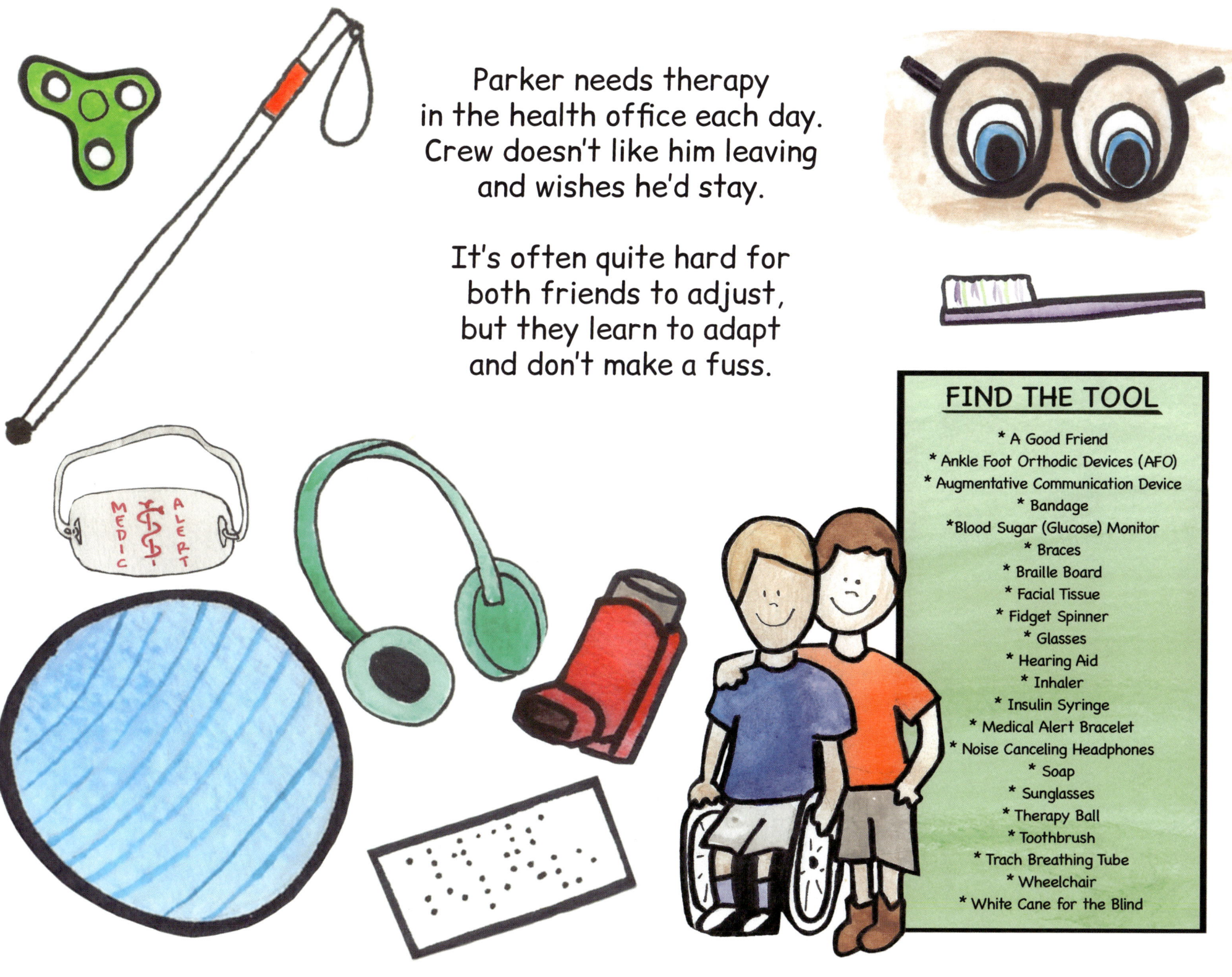

Parker needs therapy
in the health office each day.
Crew doesn't like him leaving
and wishes he'd stay.

It's often quite hard for
both friends to adjust,
but they learn to adapt
and don't make a fuss.

FIND THE TOOL

* A Good Friend
* Ankle Foot Orthodic Devices (AFO)
* Augmentative Communication Device
* Bandage
*Blood Sugar (Glucose) Monitor
* Braces
* Braille Board
* Facial Tissue
* Fidget Spinner
* Glasses
* Hearing Aid
* Inhaler
* Insulin Syringe
* Medical Alert Bracelet
* Noise Canceling Headphones
* Soap
* Sunglasses
* Therapy Ball
* Toothbrush
* Trach Breathing Tube
* Wheelchair
* White Cane for the Blind

It's time for Specials,
right before the school day ends.
They might go to music or art
where colors blend.

Excited to find out,
the class gets in line.
They head down the hall.
Parker's moving just fine.

Crew wants to help him,
and gives the wheelchair a shove.
Parker didn't need help,
but KNOWS Crew acts with love.

"Next time," he tells Crew,
"please ask to push me first.
If I need help I'll tell you.
Being shoved is the WORST!"

What is different and
what is the same?

There are so many ways
friends get to and from school.
They can walk, bike or bus.

Guess what?

Each way is cool!

Parker and Crew both
take a bus ride.
Crew climbs up the stairs
to find a seat inside.

Parker's legs can't stand up.
He can't walk up the stairs.
His bus uses a lift for
his awesome wheelchair.

The lift lowers down and
his chair rolls on slow.
Then it lifts him up,
and away the bus goes!

**What is different
and what is the same?**

After school Crew likes
to bike and to run.
Parker can also
have bicycling fun!

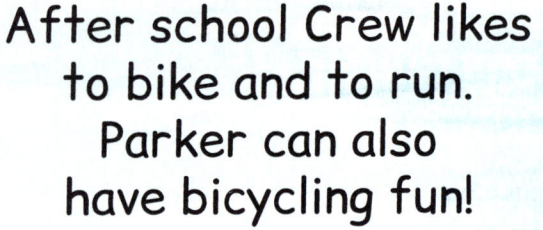

Each of Parker's legs are
secured safely with bands.

Then he pedals his bike with
his strong arms and hands.

They both love the skate park and speeding down hills.

They just make it happen with different wheels.

Crew uses a scooter to speed up and down. There are different ways to go fast, Parker has found!

What is different and what is the same?

Time for basketball practice
with Parker's team.
Crew notices quickly
that there is a theme.

Each of Parker's teammates
use a wheelchair.
Crew wants to use one too.
It doesn't seem fair.

Parker rolls over and asks
Crew to come play.
Then points to an extra chair,
making Crew's day!

They all wheel around
playing in the SAME game.
This is new fun for Crew!
He's GLAD that he came.

**What is different and
what is the same?**

When it's time for sleep
at the end of the day,
Crew and Parker both
want to stay out and play.

The time has now come
to rest and settle down.
This makes both boys sad.
They whine and they frown.

Parker has a routine and he patiently waits,
for medicine, oxygen and each leg brace.

Crew brushes his teeth
and jumps right into bed.
They both lay on their pillows
and rest their heads.

Their Mama's rock-a-bye them
and hold them tight.
Then each say their prayers for
sweet dreams through the night.

**What is different and
what is the same?**

Noticing all that's unique in each one,
Creates a life that shines bright like the sun!

Our world is a puzzle,
we're each a vital piece.
Your value can NEVER
improve or decrease.

You are loved, you are special,
despite what you do.
You're cherished and important,
BELIEVE IT,

IT'S TRUE!

Remember the example
of Parker and Crew.
Put your piece into place
and be Uniquely YOU!!

Note to Parents, Teachers & Caregivers:

Inclusion is important for all children with "special" needs, and isn't that all of us? Every person needs to recognize the ways they are similar and different from every other unique individual. Only then can we all fit together and let our unique abilities shine! The hope and prayer over this text is that it will be used as a fun, interactive way to help those in your life to see how they are different and similar to the friends in the story and the friends around them. Each page that contrasts the differences of the friends has a question off to the side to help remind the reader to ask, "What is different and what is the same?" Let the story, questions and illustrations open a dialogue that gives children and adults alike the knowledge and confidence to step forward and be a friend to everyone they encounter, inspired by their own uniqueness!

WHAT YOU SAY AND DO MATTERS!

ALWAYS:

- Refer to a person first- only refer to their impairment if pertinent. For example, if you're going to a location where navigating a wheelchair might be challenging, it might be important to say, "My friend is coming, he uses a wheelchair."
- Talk to others and ask them their name. If they don't respond THEN ask their caregiver.
- Get to know each individual- everyone is wonderfully different! Assuming things about others can keep you from connecting and making new friends!
- Use proper terminology the best that you can and become familiar with correct meanings behind terms.
- Ask questions. For example, if you see someone that wears leg braces you could ask them kindly why they need to use them.
- Recognize that others are doing their best and try to help them understand your differences!
- Remember that it is ok to do things differently in order to include everyone. Be creative! Make it a challenge to figure out a way to include all your friends in your games!
- Choose to smile at others. A smile changes everything and is so simple!

NEVER:

- Stare. Instead approach others and introduce yourself!
- Use slang to label a person. She is not a "cripple," "retarded," "disabled," or "impaired." She is simply a child with special needs.
- Refer to a person with impairment or yourself in a negative way, it can create a feeling that they/you are somehow not good enough or that something is wrong with them/you. Choose to be positive!
- Speak loudly at someone because you might think they cannot understand you. Instead, speak to them as you would anyone else, maybe you'll find a new friend!
- Be afraid to offer a helping hand. Holding a door or lending help in other loving ways is kind.
- Criticize others. Remember we are all doing the best we can and there's a good chance we do not understand the entire circumstance of others.
- Be offended when someone asks you a question. Everyone is learning. Be understanding when others approach a scenario differently than you'd have liked them to. Remember, it goes both ways! Choose kindness!

Hi, I'm Parker!

I surprised my parents on my birthday when I arrived in the world with the most severe form of Spina Bifida, called Open Myelomeningocele. Since that day I have had over 20 surgeries on my brain, spine, legs, feet, bladder, bowels, and eyes. Despite my physical challenges I am a happy, full-of-life, first grader and keep my family and friends on their toes (literally) with my wheelie popping and infectious smile! I'm obsessed with sports, especially football, and my favorite team is the Arizona State Sun Devils! My favorite sport to play is baseball at the Miracle League of Arizona! If I'm not watching or playing sports, you'll find me versing my big brother in our vibrating football game or competing in our own made-up football tournament with our collection of collegiate mini football helmets! When kids ask me questions about why I use a wheelchair, I don't mind. My favorite song says, "If you don't walk like most people do, some people walk away from you, but I won't. If you don't talk as most people do, some people talk and laugh at you, but I won't. I'll walk with you, I'll talk with you, that's how I'll show my love for you." I am really excited for the day Jesus comes again when I CAN walk, run, jump and cartwheel! Until then, I hope you'll join me in walking, talking and showing our love to everyone!

Your Friend,

Parker

Hi, I'm Crew!

I am 7 years old and one of the most curious kids around. Ask me facts about animals and I'll have lots to share!! I love playing and creating new board games. I have a huge imagination, love soccer, super heroes, performing funny songs and dance moves and doing crafts! I'm also really funny and love making people laugh! Parker and I were born a month apart into families who have been best of friends- so we've known each other since day one. Parker can't use his legs, but we still find all kinds of ways to have fun together- sometimes we have to be very creative to make it work! He has many bikes and chairs we can use too! We even like to wrestle on the carpet and he's pretty strong. I am not nervous to be friends with kids who are different than me. I try to be a good friend to everyone and you should try it too!

Your Friend,

Crew

MEET THE AUTHOR

MEET THE ILLUSTRATOR

For years, Randa Canter, even after becoming a Registered Nurse, was very timid of people who were different. Her irrational fear of walking through the blue, white and yellow painted emblem on the Disabled Parking spaces was finally defeated after growing into her role as Parker's Mom! The inspiration for "Uniquely You" came when Parker's teacher, who was getting bombarded with the curiosity of classmates invited Randa to talk with the class about his differences. She immediately felt a deep pull to share what she'd learned to be true, that every individual is unique and special and needs to be celebrated in their differences. And with that "Uniquely You" was born! Randa and her supportive, ASU football-loving husband Mike are both Arizona natives and reside in Gilbert, Arizona with their 5 dynamic and adaptable children: Ellie, Teagan, Macie, Parker & Millie. Taking bubble baths, having deep, meaningful conversations, staying active and standing on her head are a few things Randa loves! Her trademark headstands were even done on the Golden Gate Bridge and the edge of The Grand Canyon!

Amanda Kriese resides in Gilbert, Arizona with her ambitious, entrepreneurial husband Nick, their 4 active children: Carter, Kiley, Katelyn, Crew, and their talking blue-ring-neck parrot, Ava! She is very creative and has shared her artwork with close friends and family for years. Was she ever surprised when approached by her friend to illustrate a book about her son and one of his best buddies! As you can see by the gorgeous watercolor within the pages of this book, Amanda took the challenge in stride and has worked diligently to exhibit her amazing artistic talent!

Amanda is also a very passionate mother and loves to spend time with her family traveling and exploring the great outdoors: hiking, camping, bike rides, snorkeling are a few. At home she loves baking bread, making homemade strawberry jelly and caramel apples, volunteering in the community and always has a crafty project in the works.

CPSIA information can be obtained at www.ICGtesting.com
Printed in the USA
LVIW011255250320
651161LV00015B/83